Lover's Gift

RABINDRA RACHANAVALI

Lover's Gift

Rabindranath Tagore

Rupa & Co

Concept & Typeset coypyright © Rupa & Co 2002

Published 2002 by

Rupa & Co

7/16, Ansari Road, Daryaganj
New Delhi 110 002

Sales Centres:
Allahabad Bangalore Chandigarh Chennai
Dehradun Hyderabad Jaipur Kathmandu
Kolkata Ludhiana Mumbai Pune

All rights reserved.
No part of this publication may be reproduced, stored in a retrieval system, or transmitted, in any form or by any means, electronic, mechanical, photocopying, recording or otherwise, without the prior permission of the publishers.

Design & Typeset by
Arrt Creations
45 Nehru Apts, Kalkaji
New Delhi 110 019

Printed in India by
Gopsons Papers Ltd
A-14 Sector 60
Noida 201 301

page v: Painting by Rabindranath Tagore
Ink & crayon on paper. Unsigned. 25 X 31.5 cm

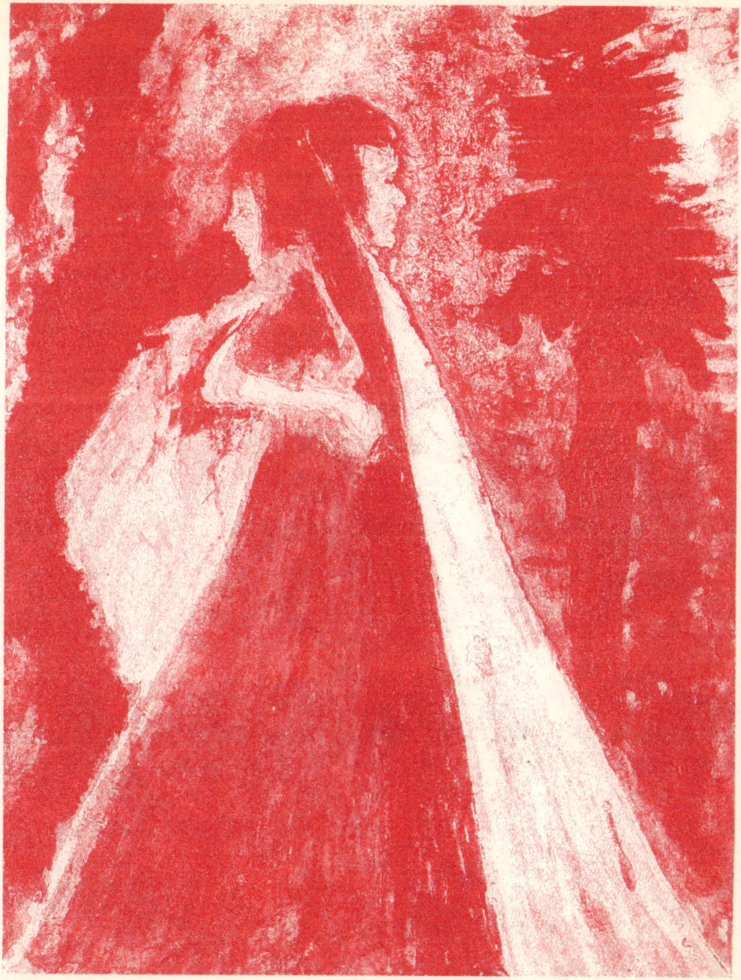

Lover's Gift

1

YOU allowed your kingly power to vanish, Shajahan, but your wish was to make imperishable a tear-drop of love.

Time has no pity for the human heart, he laughs at its sad struggle to remember.

You allured him with beauty, made him captive, and crowned the formless death with fadeless form.

The secret whispered in the hush of night to the ear of your love is wrought in the perpetual silence of stone.

Though empires crumble to dust, and centuries are lost in shadows, the marble still sighs to the stars, 'I remember.'

'I remember.' —But life forgets, for she has her call to the Endless: and she goes on her voyage unburdened, leaving her memories to the forlorn forms of beauty.

2

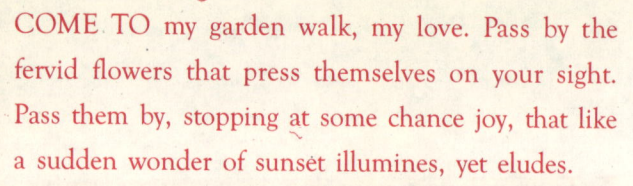

COME TO my garden walk, my love. Pass by the fervid flowers that press themselves on your sight. Pass them by, stopping at some chance joy, that like a sudden wonder of sunset illumines, yet eludes.

For love's gift is shy, it never tells its name, it flits across the shade, spreading a shiver of joy along the dust. Overtake it or miss it for ever. But a gift that can be grasped is merely a frail flower, or a lamp with a flame that will flicker.

3

THE FRUITS come in crowds into my orchard, they jostle each other. They surge up in the light in an anguish of fullness.

Proudly step into my orchard, my queen, sit there in the shade, pluck the ripe fruits from their stems, and let them yield, to the utmost, their burden of sweetness at your lips.

In my orchard the butterflies shake their wings in the sun, the leaves tremble, the fruits clamour to come to completion.

4

SHE IS near to my heart as the meadow-flower to the earth; she is sweet to me as sleep is to tired limbs. My love for her is my life flowing in its fullness, like a river in autumn flood, running with serene abandonment. My songs are one with my love, like the murmur of a stream, that sings with all its waves and currents.

5

I WOULD ask for still more, if I had the sky with all its stars, and the world with its endless riches; but I would be content with the smallest corner of this earth if only she were mine.

6

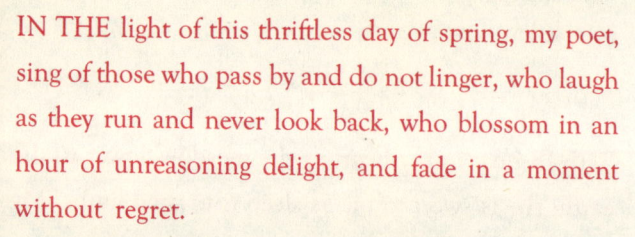

IN THE light of this thriftless day of spring, my poet, sing of those who pass by and do not linger, who laugh as they run and never look back, who blossom in an hour of unreasoning delight, and fade in a moment without regret.

Do not sit down silently, to tell the beads of your past tears and smiles,—do not stop to pick up the dropped petals from the flowers of overnight, do not go to seek things that evade you, to know the meaning that is not plain,—leave the gaps in your life where they are, for the music to come out of their depths.

7

IT IS little that remains now, the rest was spent in one careless summer. It is just enough to put in a song and sing to you; to weave in a flower-chain gently clasping your wrist; to hang in your ear like a round pink pearl, like a blushing whisper; to risk in a game one evening and utterly lose.

My boat is a frail small thing, not fit for crossing wild waves in the rain. If you but lightly step on it I shall gently row you by the shelter of the shore, where the dark water in ripples are like a dream-ruffled sleep; where the dove's cooing from the drooping branches makes the noonday shadows plaintive. At the day's end, when you are tired, I shall pluck a dripping lily to put in your hair and take my leave.

8

THERE IS ROOM for you. You are alone with your few sheaves of rice. My boat is crowded, it is heavily laden, but how can I turn you away? Your young body is slim and swaying; there is a twinkling smile in the edge of your eyes, and your robe is coloured like the rain-cloud.

The travellers will land for different roads and homes. You will sit for a while on the prow of my boat, and at the journey's end none will keep you back.

Where do you go, and to what home, to garner your sheaves? I will not question you, but when I fold my sails and moor my boat, I shall sit and wonder in the evening,—Where do you go, and to what home, to garner your sheaves?

9

WOMAN, your basket is heavy, your limbs are tired. For what distance have you set out, with what hunger of profit? The way is long and the dust is hot in the sun.

See, the lake is deep and full, its water dark like a crow's eye. The banks are sloping and tender with grass.

Dip your tired feet into the water. The noon-tide wind will pass its fingers through your hair; the pigeons will croon their sleep songs, the leaves will murmur the secrets that nestle in the shadows.

What matters it if the hours pass and the sun sets; if the way through the desolate land be lost in the waning light.

Yonder is my house, by the hedge of flowering *henna*; I will guide you. I will make a bed for you, and light a lamp. In the morning when the birds are roused by the stir of milking the cows, I will waken you.

10

WHAT IS it that drives these bees from their home; these followers of unseen trails? What cry is this in their eager wings? How can they hear the music that sleeps in the flower soul? How can they find their way to the chamber where the honey lies shy and silent?

11

IT WAS only the budding of leaves in the summer, the summer that came into the garden by the sea. It was only a stir and rustle in the south wind, a few lazy snatches of songs, and then the day was done.

But let there be flowering of love in the summer to come in the garden by the sea. Let my joy take its birth and clap its hands and dance with the surging songs, and make the morning open its eyes wide in sweet amazement.

12

AGES AGO when you opened the south gate of the garden of gods, and came down upon the first youth of the earth, O Spring; men and women rushed out of their houses, laughing and dancing, and pelting each other with flower-dust in a sudden madness of mirth.

Year-after year you bring the same flowers that you scattered in your path in that earliest April. Therefore, to-day, in their pervading perfume, they breathe the sigh of the days that are now dreams— the clinging sadness of vanished worlds. Your breeze is laden with love-legends that have faded from all human language.

One day, with fresh wonder, you came into my life that was fluttered with its first love. Since then the tender timidness of that inexperienced joy comes hidden every year in the early green buds of your lemon flowers; your red roses carry in their burning silence all that was unutterable in me: the memory of lyric hours, those days of May, rustles in the thrill of your new leaves born again and again.

13

LAST NIGHT in the garden I offered you my youth's foaming wine. You lifted the cup to your lips, you shut your eyes and smiled while I raised your veil, unbound your tresses, drawing down upon my breast your face sweet with its silence, last night when the moon's dream overflowed the world of slumber.

To-day in the dew-cooled calm of the dawn you are walking to God's temple, bathed and robed white, with a basketful of flowers in your hand. I stand aside in the shade under the tree, with my head bent, in the calm of the dawn by the lonely road to the temple.

14

IF I AM impatient to-day, forgive me, my love. It is the first summer rain, and the riverside forest is aflutter, and the blossoming *kadam* trees, are tempting the passing winds with wine-cups of perfume. See, from all corners of the sky lightnings are darting their glances, and winds are rampant in your hair.

If to-day I bring my homage to you, forgive me, my love. The everyday world is hidden in the dimness of the rain, all work has stopped in the village, the meadows are desolate. In your dark eyes the coming of the rain finds its music, and it is at your door that July waits with jasmines for your hair in its blue skirt.

15

HER NEIGHBOURS call her dark in the village— but she is a lily to my heart, yes, a lily though not fair. Light came muffled with clouds, when first I saw her in the field; her head was bare, her veil was off, her braided hair hanging loose on her neck. She may be dark as they say in the village, but I have seen her black eyes and am glad.

The pulse of the air boded storm. She rushed out of the hut, when she heard her dappled cow low in dismay. For a moment she turned her large eyes to the clouds, and felt a stir of the coming rain in the sky. I stood at the corner of the ricefield,—if she noticed me, it was known only to her (and perhaps I know it). She is dark as the message of shower in summer, dark as the shade of flowering woodland; she is dark as the longing for unknown love in the wistful night of May.

16

SHE DWELT here by the pool with its landing-stairs in ruins. Many an evening she had watched the moon made dizzy by the shaking of bamboo leaves, and on many a rainy day the smell of the wet earth had come to her over the young shoots of rice.

Her pet name is known here among those date-palm groves, and in the court-yards where girls sit and talk, while stitching their winter quilts. The water in this pool keeps in its depth the memory of her swimming limbs, and her wet feet had left their marks, day after day, on the footpath leading to the village.

The women who come to-day with their vessels to the water, have all seen her smile over simple jests, and the old peasant, taking his bullocks to their bath, used to stop at her door every day to greet her.

Many a sailing boat passes by this village; many a traveller takes rest beneath that banyan tree; the ferry boat crosses to yonder ford carrying crowds to the market; but they never notice this spot by the village road, near the pool with its ruined landing-stairs,— where dwelt she whom I love.

17

WHILE AGES passed and the bees haunted the summer gardens, the moon smiled to the lilies of the night, the lightnings flashed their fiery kisses to the clouds and fled laughing, the poet stood in a corner, one with the trees and clouds. He kept his heart silent, like a flower, watched through his dreams as does the crescent moon; and wandered like the summer breeze for no purpose.

One April evening, when the moon rose up like a bubble from the depth of the sunset; and one maiden was busy watering the plants; and one feeding her doe, and one making her peacock dance, the poet broke out singing,—'O listen to the secrets of the world. I know that the lily is pale for the moon's love. The lotus draws her veil aside before the morning sun, and the reason is simple if you think. The meaning of the bee's hum in the ear of the early jasmine has escaped the learned, but the poet knows.'

The sun went down in a blaze of blush, the moon loitered behind the trees, and the south wind whispered to the lotus, that the poet was not as simple as he seemed. The maidens and youths clapped their hands and cried,—'The world's secret is out.' They looked into each other's eyes and sang—'Let our secret as well be flung into the winds.'

18

YOUR DAYS will be full of cares, if you must give me your heart. My house by the cross-roads has its doors open and my mind is absent,—for I sing.

I shall never be made to answer for it, if you must give me your heart. If I pledge my word to you in tunes now, and am too much in earnest to keep it when music is silent, you must forgive me; for the law laid in May is best broken in December.

Do not always keep remembering it, if you must give me your heart. When your eyes sing with love, and your voice ripples with laughter, my answers to your questions will be wild, and not miserly accurate in facts,—they are to be believed for ever and then forgotten for good.

19

IT IS written in the book, that Man, when fifty, must leave the noisy world, to go to the forest seclusion. But the poet proclaims that only for the young is the forest hermitage. For it is the birth-place of flowers, and the haunt of birds and bees; and hidden nooks are waiting there for the thrill of lover's whispers. There the moonlight, that is all one kiss for the *malati* flowers, has its deep message, but those who understand it are far below fifty.

And alas, youth is inexperienced and wilful, therefore it is but meet, that the old should take charge of the household, and the young take to the seclusion of forest shades, and the severe discipline of courting.

20

WHERE IS the market for you, my song? Is it there where the learned muddle the summer breeze with their snuff; where dispute is unending if the oil depend upon the cask, or the cask upon the oil; where yellow manuscripts frown upon the fleet-footed frivolousness of life? My song cries out, Ah, no, no, no.

Where is the market for you, my song? Is it there where the man of fortune grows enormous in pride and flesh in his marble palace, with his books on the shelves, dressed in leather, painted in gold, dusted by slaves, their virgin pages dedicated to the god obscure? My song gasped and said, Ah, no, no, no.

Where is the market for you, my song? Is it there where the young student sits, with his head bent upon his books, and his mind straying in youth's dreamland; where prose is prowling on the desk, and poetry hiding in the heart? There among that dusty disorder would you care to play hide-and-seek? My song remains silent in shy hesitation.

Where is the market for you, my song? Is it there where the bride is busy in the house, where she runs to her bedroom the moment she is free, and snatches, from under her pillows, the book of romance so roughly handled by the baby, so full of the scent of her hair? My song heaves a sigh and trembles with uncertain desire.

Where is the market for you, my song? Is it there where the least of a bird's notes is never missed, where the stream's babbling finds its full wisdom, where all the lute-strings of the world shower their music upon two fluttering hearts? My song bursts out and cries, Yes, yes.

21

(From the Bengali of Devendranath Sen)

METHINKS, my love, before the daybreak of life you stood under some waterfall of happy dreams, filling your blood with its liquid turbulence. Or, perhaps, your path was through the garden of the gods, where the merry multitude of jasmine, lilies, and oleanders fell in your arms in heaps, and entering your heart became boisterous.

Your laughter is a song whose words are drowned in the clamour of tune, a rapture of odour of flowers that are not seen; it is like the moonlight breaking through your lips' window when the moon is hiding in your heart. I ask for no reason, I forget the cause, I only know that your laughter is the tumult of insurgent life.

22

I SHALL gladly suffer the pride of culture to die out in my house, if only in some fortunate future I am born a herd boy in the Brinda forest.

The herd boy who grazes his cattle sitting under the banyan tree, and idly weaves *gunja* flowers into garlands, who loves to splash and plunge in the Jamuna's cool deep stream.

He calls his companions to wake up when morning dawns, and all the houses in the lane hum with the sound of the churn, clouds of dust are raised by the cattle, the maidens come out in the courtyard to milk the kine.

As the shadows deepen under the *tomal* trees, and the dusk gathers on the river-banks; when the milkmaids, while crossing the turbulent water tremble with fear; and loud peacocks, with tails outspread, dance in the forest, he watches the summer clouds.

When the April night is sweet as a fresh-blown flower, he disappears in the forest with a peacock's plume in his hair; the swing ropes are twined with flowers on the branches; the south wind throbs with music, and the merry shepherd boys crowd on the banks of the blue river.

No, I will never be the leader, brothers, of this new age of new Bengal; I shall not trouble to light the lamp of culture for the benighted. If only I could be born, under the shady Ashoka groves, in some village of Brinda, where milk is churned by the maidens.

23

I LOVED the sandy bank where, in the lonely pools, ducks clamoured and turtles basked in the sun; where, with evening, stray fishing-boats took shelter in the shadow by the tall grass.

You loved the wooded bank where shadows were gathered in the arms of the bamboo thickets; where women came with their vessels through the winding lane.

The same river flowed between us, singing the same song to both its banks. I listened to it, lying alone on the sand under the stars; and you listened sitting by the edge of the slope in the early morning light. Only the words I heard from it you did not know and the secret it spoke to you was a mystery for ever to me.

24

YOUR WINDOW half opened and veil half raised you stand there waiting for the bangle-seller to come with his tinsel. You idly watch the heavy cart creak on in the dusty road, and the boat-mast crawling along the horizon across the far-off river.

The world to you is like an old woman's chant at her spinning-wheel, unmeaning rhymes crowded with random images.

But who knows if he is on his way this lazy sultry noon, the Stranger, carrying his basket of strange wares.

He will pass by your door with his clear cry, and you shall fling open your window, cast off your veil, come out of the dusk of your dreams and meet your destiny.

25

I CLASP your hands, and my heart plunges into the dark of your eyes, seeking you, who ever evade me behind words and silence.

Yet I know that I must be content in my love, with what is fitful and fugitive. For we have met for a moment in the crossing of the roads. Have I the power to carry you through this crowd of worlds, through this maze of paths? Have I the food that can sustain you, across the dark passage gaping with arches of death?

26

IF, BY chance you think of me, I shall sing to you when the rainy evening loosens her shadows upon the

Lover's Gift • 21

river, slowly trailing her dim light towards the west,—when the day's remnant is too narrow for work or for play.

You will sit alone in the balcony of the south, and I shall sing from the darkened room. In the growing dusk, the smell of the wet leaves will come through the window; and the stormy winds will become clamorous in the coconut grove.

When the lighted lamp is brought into the room I shall go. And then, perhaps, you will listen to the night, and hear my song when I am silent.

27

I FILLED my tray with whatever I had, and gave it to you. What shall I bring to your feet tomorrow, I wonder. I am like the tree that, at the end of the flowering summer, gazes at the sky with its lifted branches bare of their blossoms.

But in all my past offerings is there not a single flower made fadeless by the eternity of tears?

Will you remember it and thank me with your eyes when I stand before you with empty hands at the leave-taking of my summer days?

28

I DREAMT that she sat by my head, tenderly ruffling my hair with her fingers, playing the melody of her touch. I looked at her face and struggled with my tears, till the agony of unspoken words burst my sleep like a bubble.

I sat up and saw the glow of the milky way above my window, like a world of silence on fire, and I wondered if at this moment she had a dream that rhymed with mine.

29

I THOUGHT I had something to say to her when our eyes met across the hedge. But she passed away. And it rocks day and night, like a boat, on every wave of the hours the word that I had to say to her. It seems to sail in the autumn clouds in an endless quest and to bloom into evening flowers seeking its lost moment in the sunset. It twinkles like fireflies in my heart to find its meaning in the dusk of despair the word that I had to say to her.

30

THE SPRING flowers break out like the passionate pain of unspoken love. With their breath comes the memory of my old day songs. My heart of a sudden has put on green leaves of desire. My love came not but her touch is in my limbs, and her voice comes across the fragrant fields. Her gaze is in the sad depth of the sky, but where are her eyes? Her kisses flit in the air, but where are her lips?

A Posy

(From the Bengali of Satyendranath Datta)

MY flowers were like milk and honey and wine; I bound them into a posy with a golden ribbon, but they escaped my watchful care and fled away and only the ribbon remains.

My songs were like milk and honey and wine, they were held in the rhythm of my beating heart, but they spread their wings and fled away, the darlings of the idle hours, and my heart beats in silence.

The beauty I loved was like milk and honey and wine, her lips like the rose of the dawn, her eyes bee-black. I kept my heart silent lest it should startle her, but she eluded me like my flowers and like my songs, and my love remains alone.

32

MANY A TIME when the spring day knocked at our door I kept busy with my work and you did not answer. Now when I am left alone and heartsick the spring day comes once again, but I know not how to turn him away from the door. When he came to crown us with joy the gate was shut, but now when he comes with his gift of sorrow his path must be open.

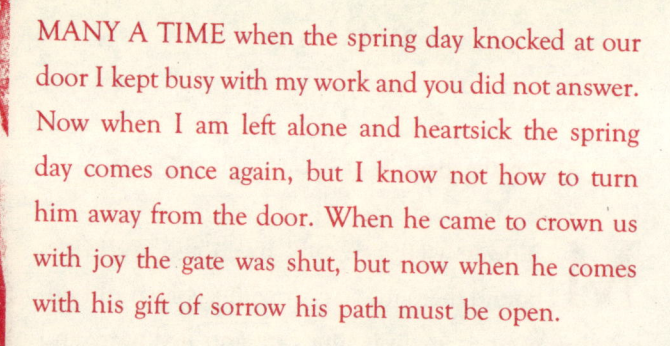

33

THE BOISTEROUS spring, who once came into my life with its lavish laughter, burdening her hours with improvident roses, setting skies aflame with the red kisses of new-born *ashoka* leaves, now comes stealing into my solitude through the lonely lanes along the brooding shadows heavy with silence, and sits still in my balcony gazing across the fields, where the green of the earth swoons exhausted in the utter paleness of the sky.

WHEN OUR farewell moment came, like a low-hanging rain cloud, I had only time to tie a red ribbon on your wrist, while my hands trembled. Today I sit alone on the grass in the season of *mahua* flowers, with one quivering question in my mind, 'Do you still keep the little red ribbon tied on your wrist?'

You went by the narrow road that skirted the blossoming field of flax. I saw that my garland of overnight was still hanging loose from your hair. But why did you not wait till I could gather, in the morning, new flowers for my final gift? I wonder if unaware it dropped on your way,—the garland hanging loose from your hair.

Many a song I had sung to you, morning and evening, and the last one you carried in your voice when you went away. You never tarried to hear the one song unsung I had for you alone and for ever. I wonder if, at last, you are tired of my song that you hummed to yourself while walking through the field.

35

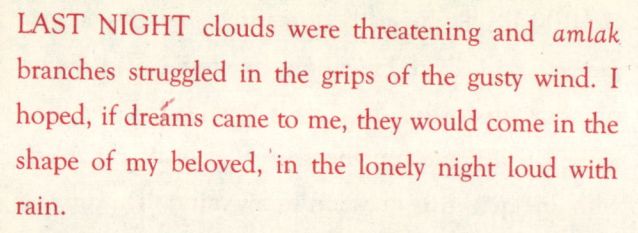

LAST NIGHT clouds were threatening and *amlak* branches struggled in the grips of the gusty wind. I hoped, if dreams came to me, they would come in the shape of my beloved, in the lonely night loud with rain.

The winds still moan through the fields, and the tear-stained cheeks of dawn are pale. My dreams have been in vain, for truth is hard, and dreams, too, have their own ways.

Last night when the darkness was drunken with storm, and the rain, like night's veil, was torn by the winds into shreds, would it make truth jealous, if untruth came to me in the shape of my beloved, in the starless night loud with rain?

36

MY FETTERS, you made music in my heart. I played with you all day long and made you my ornament. We were the best of friends, my fetters. There were times when I was afraid of you, but my fear made me love you the more. You were companions of my long dark night, and I make my bow to you, before I bid you good-bye, my fetters.

37

YOU HAD your rudder broken many a time, my boat, and your sails torn to tatters. Often had you drifted towards the sea, dragging anchor and heeded not. But now there has spread a crack in your hull and your hold is heavy. Now is the time for you to end your voyage, to be rocked into sleep by the lapping of the water by the beach.

Alas, I know all warning is vain. The veiled face of dark doom lures you. The madness of the storm and the waves is upon you. The music of the tide is rising high. You are shaken by the fever of that dance.

Then break your chain, my boat, and be free, and fearlessly rush to your wreck.

Lover's Gift • 29

38

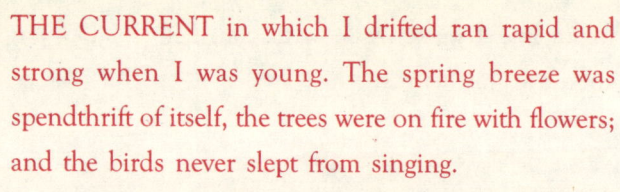

THE CURRENT in which I drifted ran rapid and strong when I was young. The spring breeze was spendthrift of itself, the trees were on fire with flowers; and the birds never slept from singing.

I sailed with giddy speed, carried away by the flood of passion; I had no time to see and feel and take the world into my being.

Now that youth has ebbed and I am stranded on the bank, I can hear the deep music of all things, and the sky opens to me its heart of stars.

39

THERE IS a looker-on who sits behind my eyes. It seems he has seen things in ages and worlds beyond memory's shore, and those forgotten sights glisten on the grass, and shiver on the leaves. He has seen under new veils the face of the one beloved, in twilight hours of many a nameless star. Therefore his sky seems to ache with the pain of countless meetings and partings, and a longing pervades this spring breeze,—the longing that is full of the whisper of ages without beginning.

40

A MESSAGE came from my youth of vanished days, saying, 'I wait for you among the quiverings of unborn May, where smiles ripen for tears and hours ache with songs unsung.'

It says, 'Come to me across the worn-out track of age, through the gates of death. For dreams fade, hopes fail, the gathered fruits of the year decay, but I am the eternal truth, and you shall meet me again and again in your voyage of life from shore to shore.'

41

THE GIRLS are out to fetch water from the river—their laughter comes through the trees, I long to join them in the lane, where goats graze in the shade, and squirrels flit from sun to shadow, across the fallen leaves.

But my day's task is already done, my jars are filled. I stand at my door to watch the glistening green of the *areca* leaves, and hear the laughing women going to fetch water from the river.

It has ever been dear to me to carry the burden of my full vessel day after day, in the dew-dipped morning freshness and in the tired glimmer of the dayfall.

Its gurgling water babbled to me when my mind was idle, it laughed with the silent laughter of my joyous thoughts—it spoke to my heart with tearful sobs when I was sad. I have carried it in stormy days, when the loud rain drowned the anxious cooing of doves.

My day's task is done, my jars are filled, the light wanes in the west, and shadows gather beneath the trees; a sigh comes from the flowering linseed field, and my wistful eyes follow the lane, that runs through the village to the bank of the dark water.

ARE YOU a mere picture, and not as true as those stars, true as this dust? They throb with the pulse of things, but you are immensely aloof in your stillness, painted form.

The day was when you walked with me, your breath warm, your limbs singing of life. My world found its speech in your voice, and touched my heart with your face. You suddenly stopped in your walk, in the shadow-side of the Forever, and I went on alone.

Life, like a child, laughs, shaking its rattle of death as it runs; it beckons me on, I follow the unseen; but you stand there, where you stopped behind that dust and those stars; and you are a mere picture.

No, it cannot be. Had the lifeflood utterly stopped in you, it would stop the river in its flow, and the footfall of dawn in her cadence of colours. Had the glimmering dusk of your hair vanished in the hopeless dark, the woodland shade of summer would die with its dreams.

Can it be true that I forgot you? We haste on without heed, forgetting the flowers on the roadside hedge. Yet they breathe unaware into our forgetfulness, filling it with music. You have moved from my world, to take seat at the root of my life, and therefore is this forgetting—remembrance lost in its own depth.

You are no longer before my songs, but one with them. You came to me with the first ray of dawn. I lost you with the last gold of evening. Ever since I am always finding you through the dark. No, you are no mere picture.

43

DYING, YOU have left behind you the great sadness of the Eternal in my life. You have painted my thought's horizon with the sunset colours of your departure, leaving a track of tears across the earth to love's heaven. Clasped in your dear arms, life and death united in me in a marriage bond.

I think I can see you watching there in the balcony with your lamp lighted, where the end and the beginning of all things meet. My world went hence through the doors that you opened—you holding the cup of death to my lips, filling it with life from your own.

44

WHEN IN your death you died to all that was outside me, vanishing from the thousand things of the world, to be fully reborn in my sorrow, I felt that my life had grown perfect, the man and the woman becoming one in me for ever.

45

BRING BEAUTY and order into my forlorn life, woman, as you brought them into my house when you lived. Sweep away the dusty fragments of the hours, fill the empty jars and mend all neglects. Then open the inner door of the shrine, light the candle, and let us meet there in silence before our God.

46

THE SKY gazes on its own endless blue and dreams. We clouds are its whims, we have no home. The stars shine on the crown of Eternity. Their records are permanent, while ours are penciled, to be rubbed off the next moment. Our part is to appear on the stage of the air to sound our tambourines and fling flashes of laughter. But from our laughter comes the rain, which is real enough, and thunder which is no jest. Yet we have no claim upon Time for wages, and the breath that blew us into being blows us away before we are given a name.

47

THE ROAD is my wedded companion. She speaks to me under my feet all day, she sings to my dreams all night.

My meeting with her had no beginning, it begins endlessly at each daybreak, renewing its summer in fresh flowers and songs, and her every new kiss is the first kiss to me.

The road and I are lovers. I change my dress for her night after night, leaving the tattered cumber of the old in the wayside inns when the day dawns.

48

I TRAVELLED the old road every day, I took my fruits to the market, my cattle to the meadows, I ferried my boat across the stream and all the ways were well known to me.

One morning my basket was heavy with wares. Men were busy in the fields, the pastures crowded with cattle; the breast of earth heaved with the mirth of ripening rice.

Suddenly there was a tremor in the air, and the sky seemed to kiss me on my forehead. My mind started up like the morning out of mist.

I forgot to follow the track. I stepped a few paces from the path, and my familiar world appeared strange to me, like a flower I had only known in bud.

My everyday wisdom was ashamed. I went astray in the fairyland of things. It was the best luck of my life, that I lost my path that morning, and found my eternal childhood.

49

WHERE IS heaven? you ask me, my child,—the sages tell us it is beyond the limits of birth and death, unswayed by the rhythm of day and night; it is not of this earth.

But your poet knows that its eternal hunger is for time and space, and it strives evermore to be born in the fruitful dust. Heaven is fulfilled in your sweet body, my child, in your palpitating heart.

The sea is beating its drums in joy, the flowers are a-tiptoe to kiss you. For heaven is born in you, in the arms of the mother-dust.

The Child

(Translated from the Bengali of Dwijendralal Roy)

'COME, moon, come down, kiss my darling on the forehead,' cries the mother as she holds the baby girl in her lap while the moon smiles as it dreams. There come stealing in the dark the vague fragrance of the summer and the night-bird's songs from the shadow-laden solitude of the mango-grove. At a far-away village rises from a peasant's flute a fountain of plaintive notes, and the young mother, sitting on the terrace, baby in her lap, croons sweetly, 'Come, moon, come down, kiss my darling on the forehead.' Once she looks up at the light of the sky, and then at the light of the earth in her arms, and I wonder at the placid silence of the moon.

The baby laughs and repeats her mother's call, 'Come, moon, come down.' The mother smiles, and smiles the moonlit night, and I, the poet, the husband of the baby's mother, watch this picture from behind, unseen.

51

THE EARLY autumn day is cloudless. The river is full to the brim, washing the naked roots of the tottering tree by the ford. The long narrow path, like the thirsty tongue of the village, dips down into the stream.

My heart is full, as I look around me and see the silent sky and the flowing water, and feel that happiness is spread abroad, as simply as a smile on a child's face.

52

TIRED OF waiting, you burst your bonds, impatient flowers, before the winter had gone. Glimpses of the unseen comer reached your wayside watch, and you rushed out running and panting, impulsive jasmines, troops of riotous roses.

You were the first to march to the breach of death, your clamour of colour and perfume troubled the air. You laughed and pressed and pushed each other, bared your breast and dropped in heaps.

The Summer will come in its time, sailing in the floodtide of the south wind. But you never counted slow moments to be sure of him. You recklessly spent your all in the road, in the terrible joy of faith.

You heard his footsteps from afar, and flung your mantle of death for him to tread upon. Your bonds break even before the rescuer is seen, you make him your own ere he can come and claim you.

Champa

(Translated from the Bengali of Satyendranath Datta)

I opened my bud when April breathed her last and the summer scorched with kisses the unwilling earth. I came half afraid and half curious, like a mischievous imp peeping at a hermit's cell.

I heard the frightened whispers of the despoiled woodland, and the *Kokil* gave voice to the languor of the summer; through the fluttering leaf curtain of my birth-chamber I saw the world grim, grey, and haggard.

Yet boldly I came out strong with the faith of youth, quaffed the fiery wine from the glowing bowl of the sky, and proudly saluted the morning, I, the champa flower, who carry the perfume of the sun in my heart.

54

IN THE BEGINNING of time, there rose from the churning of God's dream two women. One is the dancer at the court of paradise, the desired of men, she who laughs and plucks the minds of the wise from their cold meditations and of fools from their emptiness; and scatters them like seeds with careless hands in the extravagant winds of March, in the flowering frenzy of May.

The other is the crowned queen of heaven, the mother, throned on the fullness of golden autumn; she who in the harvest-time brings straying hearts to the smile sweet as tears, the beauty deep as the sea of silence,—brings them to the temple of the Unknown, at the holy confluence of Life and Death.

55

THE NOONDAY air is quivering, like gauzy wings of a dragon-fly. Roofs of the village huts brood birdlike over the drowsy households, while a *Kokil* sings unseen from its leafy loneliness.

The fresh liquid notes drop upon the tuneless toil of the human crowd, adding music to lovers' whispers, to mothers' kisses, to children's laughter. They flow over our thoughts, like a stream over pebbles, rounding them in beauty every unconscious moment.

56

THE EVENING was lonely for me, and I was reading a book till my heart became dry, and it seemed to me that beauty was a thing fashioned by the traders in words. Tired I shut the book and snuffed the candle. In a moment the room was flooded with moonlight.

Spirit of Beauty, how could you, whose radiance overbrims the sky, stand hidden behind a candle's tiny flame? How could a few vain words from a book rise like a mist, and veil her whose voice has hushed the heart of earth into ineffable calm?

57

This autumn is mine, for she was rocked in my heart. The glistening bells of her anklets rang in my blood, and her misty veil fluttered in my breath. I know the touch of her blown hair in all my dreams. She is abroad in the trembling leaves that danced in my life-throbs, and her eyes that smile from the blue sky drank their light from me.

58

THINGS THRONG and laugh loud in the sky; the sands and dust dance and whirl like children. Man's mind is aroused by their shouts; his thoughts long to be the playmates of things.

Our dreams, drifting in the stream of the vague, stretch their arms to clutch the earth,—their efforts stiffen into bricks and stones, and thus the city of man is built.

Voices come swarming from the past,—seeking answers from the living moments. Beats of their wings fill the air with tremulous shadows, and sleepless thoughts in our minds leave their nests to take flight across the desert of dimness, in the passionate thirst for forms. They are lampless pilgrims, seeking the shore of light, to find themselves in things. They will be lured into poet's rhymes, they will be housed in the towers of the town not yet planned, they have their call to arms from the battlefields of the future, they are bidden to join hands in the strifes of peace yet to come.

59

THEY DO not build high towers in the Land of All-I-Have-Found. A grassy lawn runs by the road, with a stream of fugitive water at its side. The bees haunt the cottage porches abloom with passion flowers. The men set out on their errands with a smile, and in the evening they come home with a song, with no wages, in the Land of All-I-Have-Found.

In the midday, sitting in the cool of their courtyards, the women hum and spin at their wheels, while over the waving harvest comes wafted the music of shepherds' flutes. It rejoices the wayfarers' hearts who walk singing through the shimmering shadows of the fragrant forest in the Land of All-I-Have-Found.

The traders sail with their merchandise down the river, but they do not moor their boats in this land; soldiers march with banners flying, but the king never stops his chariot. Travellers who come from afar to rest here awhile, go away without knowing what there is in the Land of All-I-Have-Found.

Here crowds do not jostle each other in the roads. O poet, set up your house in this land. Wash from your feet the dust of distant wanderings, tune your lute, and at the day's end stretch yourself on the cool grass under the evening star in the Land of All-I-Have-Found.

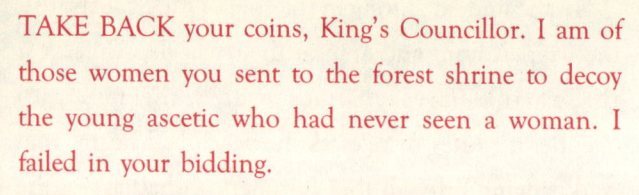

TAKE BACK your coins, King's Councillor. I am of those women you sent to the forest shrine to decoy the young ascetic who had never seen a woman. I failed in your bidding.

Dimly day was breaking when the hermit boy came to bathe in the stream, his tawny locks crowded on his shoulders, like a cluster of morning clouds, and his limbs shining like a streak of sunbeam. We laughed and sang as we rowed in our boat; we jumped into the river in a mad frolic, and danced around him, when the sun rose staring at us from the water's edge in a flush of divine anger.

Like a child-god, the boy opened his eyes and watched our movements, the wonder deepening till his eyes shone like morning stars. He lifted his clasped hands and chanted a hymn of praise in his bird-like young voice, thrilling every leaf of the forest. Never such words were sung to a mortal woman before; they were like the silent hymn to the dawn which rises from the hushed hills. The women hid their mouths with their hands, their bodies swaying with laughter, and a spasm of doubt ran across his face. Quickly came I to his side, sorely pained, and, bowing to his feet, I said, 'Lord, accept my service.'

I led him to the grassy bank, wiped his body with the end of my silken mantle, and, kneeling on the ground, I dried his feet with my trailing hair. When I raised my face and looked into his eyes, I thought I felt the world's first kiss to the first woman,—Blessed am I, blessed is God, who made me a woman. I heard him say to me, 'What God unknown are you? Your touch is the touch of the Immortal, your eyes have the mystery of the midnight.'

Ah, no, not that smile, King's Councillor,—the dust of worldly wisdom has covered your sight, old man. But this boy's innocence pierced the mist and saw the shining truth, the woman divine.

Ah, how the goddess wakened in me, at the awful light of that first adoration. Tears filled my eyes, the morning ray caressed my hair like a sister, and the woodland breeze kissed my forehead as it kisses the flowers.

The women clapped their hands, and laughed their obscene laugh, and with veils dragging on the dust and hair hanging loose, they began to pelt him with flowers.

Alas, my spotless sun, could not my shame weave fiery mist to cover you in its folds? I fell at his feet and cried, 'Forgive me.' I fled like a stricken deer through shade and sun, and cried as I fled, 'Forgive me.' The women's foul laughter pressed me like a crackling fire, but the words ever rang in my ears, 'What God unknown are you?'